I0189856

All You Need

Love: Coloring Book for Adults

MantraCraft™

Copyright © 2020 by MantraCraft

All rights reserved. No part of this publication may be reproduced, distributed, or transmitted in any form or by any means, including photocopying, recording, or other electronic or mechanical methods.

Sweet love

This Coloring Book belongs to:

_____

_____

_____

_____

Color Test Page

Love

You make me happy

You are so LOVED

I LIKE YOU
I LOVE YOU

Sweet love

Valentine`s Day

I Love You to the Moon and Back

I LOVE YOU

All you need is love

You are the Best

for You with LOVE

Because
of
Love

True Love Never Ends

Stay beautiful

www.ingramcontent.com/pod-product-compliance
Lightning Source LLC
Chambersburg PA
CBHW081216020426
42331CB00012B/3037